Six tracks about knowing God

Contributors :

Terry Dunnell
Andrew Graystone
Chris Powell

Scripture Union
130 City Road, London EC1V 2NJ

Serendipity UK
48 Peterborough Road, London SW6 3EB

In this series....

Going live   —   Living for God   (ISBN 0 86201 668 1)

Tuned in   —   Knowing God   (ISBN 0 86201 670 3)

Sounds like me   —   Am I OK?   (ISBN 0 86201 665 7)

Making contact   —   Living with others   (ISBN 0 86201 666 5)

System breakdown —   What's gone wrong?   (ISBN 0 86201 669 X)

Power supply   —   Power for good – power for evil   (ISBN 0 86201 667 3)

©   Serendipity UK   1990
First published 1990
ISBN 0 86201 670 3

British Library Cataloguing in Publication Data
Dunnell, Terry
     Tuned In: knowing God.
     1. Young people. Christian life
     I. Title II. Graystone, Andrew III. Powell,
Chris IV. Series
     248 83

Printed by Ebenezer Baylis and Son Limited,
The Trinity Press, Worcester and London.

Acknowledgements
Cover design and artwork: Adept Design.
Internal artwork: Pauline Adams.
Series editor: Andrew Graystone.
Photograph by Gordon Gray.

Contents

Instructions

 means do this bit by yourself.

 means choose a partner and work together.

 means discuss this with the whole group.

Before you start...

Before using one of the tracks in this book, read the notes on page 44 and the advice on specific tracks on pages 46 to 48.

Why bother

LOAD

It was the sixth week of the summer holiday and Marcus was bored. I mean *very* bored. He was so bored he thought about reading the telephone directory to pass the time. He looked up at his other books ranged along the shelves. There was the instruction book for his computer, *PCW 8256 – A User's Guide*. But he knew it all now. Next to it was *Ten Tales for Boys*. Yuk! Why did his uncle always give him stuff that a five year old would like? Then there were a couple of old *Shoot* annuals that he'd read hundreds of times.

On the next shelf there was *The Secret Diary of Adrian Mole*, two poetry books that Karen had given him when they were going out, and *The History of Great Britain* which he'd forgotten to give in at the end of the third year. Not exactly a great read. There was only one thing for it. He could sit here and die of boredom, or else....

He took down the old Bible from the top shelf. He lay on his bed and looked at it. There was a thick layer of dust on the cover, and he wrote BORING in big letters with his finger. According to Mum, his granny had given it to him when he was born. Stupid present for a baby.

Inside the front cover his granny had written something in her scrawly handwriting. He could only make out a few words. There was his name, and something about '...this book God will tell you...' and then '...you should follow...'

Marcus thought about his granny, who had always been nice to him. The book was heavy and its leathery covers reminded him of the way her hands used to feel.

He let the book fall open near the middle and looked for a good bit.

with the Bible ?

GROUP What do you think Marcus' granny had written in the front of his Bible? Choose words to go in the spaces:

- - - - - - - - - - - - - - - - *this book*

God will tell you - - - - - - - - - - -

- - - - - - - - - - - - - - - *you should*

follow - - - - - - - - - - -

GROUP Which of Marcus' other books do you think has most in common with his Bible?

Ten Tales for Boys because

....

A User's Guide for his computer because

....

The *Shoot* annuals because

....

The Secret Diary of Adrian Mole because

....

The poetry books because

....

The History of Great Britain because

....

TWOS Why do you think Marcus' granny might have given him a Bible when he was a baby?

TWOS People sometimes say that God speaks to them through the Bible. What do you think they might mean by this?

SOLO Here are some things that people have said about the Bible. Cross out the statements that you think are *not* true.

The Bible is....

 ....boring
 ....hard to understand
 ....exciting
 ....God's way of telling me about himself
 ....full of mistakes and contradictions
 ....the book I read more than any other
 ....just like any other old book

GROUP **Welcome!** As you start on this booklet it would be good to make everybody feel welcome in the group. Take a moment for everybody to walk round the room and welcome everybody else with a handshake or hug, whichever is appropriate. Do this even if you know each other well already.

STOP

What does God have to say about the Bible ?

- Read the Bible passages.
- Mark any discoveries you make.
- Jot down any questions you are left with.
- Talk about your discoveries and questions with the group.....

In what ways is the Bible like a mirror?

PLAY

When Paul was in prison he wrote this in a letter to his young friend Timothy. He wanted to tell Timothy why it was important for him to read the Bible.

Lots of books say wise things. What's so special about the Bible?

According to Paul, what's the point of reading the Bible?

Continue in the truths that you were taught and firmly believe. You know who your teachers were, and you remember that ever since you were a child, you have known the Holy Scriptures, which are able to give you the wisdom that leads to salvation through faith in Christ Jesus. All Scripture is inspired by God and is useful for teaching the truth, rebuking error, correcting faults, and giving instruction for right living, so that the person who serves God may be fully qualified and equipped to do every kind of good deed.

2 Timothy 3:14–17

According to James there are two ways of responding to what we read in the Bible. What are they?

This bit is from a letter too. This time it was written by James. He wanted Christians everywhere to know that there was no point in reading the Bible and hearing God's word if you didn't go on to act on it.

Do not deceive yourselves by just listening to his [God's] word; instead, put it into practice. Whoever listens to the word but does not put it into practice is like a man who looks into a mirror and sees himself as he is. He takes a good look at himself and then goes away and at once forgets what he looks like. But whoever looks closely into the perfect law that sets people free, who keeps on paying attention to it and does not simply listen and then forget it, but puts it into practice – that person will be blessed by God in what he does.

James 1:22–25

scripture, n. Another word for the Bible.

How can we do this? How can we avoid just reading the Bible and forgetting what it says?

FAST FORWARD

TWOS According to the passages you have just read, why did God give us the Bible? (Tick one or more.)

For bedtime stories to help us get to
sleep ❑

To tell us about Jesus and his love
for us ❑

To make us feel bad about ourselves ❑

As an instruction manual for the world ❑

To give us a list of rules and penalties ❑

So teachers can quote from it in
assembly ❑

So that the good news of Jesus would
not be forgotten ❑

To make us wise about ourselves ❑

Other ....

TWOS James says we should 'look closely' into God's word. Here are some ways you could do that. Give them points out of ten according to how helpful you think they would be. (1 = useless, 10 = very helpful.)

Use a microscope ......

Read a bit each day ......

Get hold of some Bible study notes ......

Read the Bible in the original Greek
and Hebrew ......

Ask God to help you to understand it ......

Open the Bible in the middle and look
for a good bit ......

Get hold of a version in modern English ......

Start at page one and read to the end ......

Read the Bible with a friend or in a
group ......

GROUP Has anyone in the group tried any of the ideas above? If someone wanted to read the Bible how would you recommend them to do it? Is there anything you would recommend them not to do?

TWOS Fill in the gaps in this passage by choosing words from the box below or adding your own.

Reading the Bible is .... for a Christian because it is the way God tells us

about Jesus. It is .... to read

from it regularly, and it is ....
to read from a version you can understand.

Important • Helpful • Vital • Easy • Hard
Dangerous • Impossible • Funny • Exciting

SOLO Put an X on the lines below.

I find reading the Bible by myself
Easy _____ *Difficult*

I find reading the Bible with this group
Easy _____ *Difficult*

Share your answers with a friend.

How could this group help you to read and understand the Bible? Why not ask them now?

WHAT WILL YOU DO?

A group of your friends are having an argument about how the world began. One of them says that she believes God made the world in seven days just like the Bible says. But another says that's rubbish because everyone knows the world evolved. What will you do?

TOUGH TALKING

What does it mean for Paul to say that the Bible is 'inspired' by God? Did God tell the writers the actual words he wanted them to put? Or did he just give them the ideas? Or what?

Does God speak to us in other ways apart from the Bible? Could he ever say something that contradicted what was in the Bible?

GOING FURTHER

If you want to think more about the Bible, check out these Bible passages :

2 Peter 1:16–21 – An eyewitness account

Psalm 19:7–14 – The law of the Lord

Matthew 4:1–11 – How Jesus used the Bible

||PAUSE||

Psalm 19 is about how God speaks to us through his creation and through his word. Divide into two groups and say this Psalm together, each group reading alternate phrases.

The law of the LORD is perfect;
  it gives new strength.
*The commands of the LORD are
    trustworthy,
  giving wisdom to those who lack it.*
The laws of the LORD are right,
  and those who obey them are
    happy.
*The commands of the LORD are just
  and give understanding to the mind.*
Reverence for the LORD is good;
  it will continue for ever.
*The judgements of the LORD are just;
  they are always fair.*
They are more desirable than the finest
    gold;
  they are sweeter than the purest
    honey.
*They give knowledge to me, your
    servant;
  I am rewarded for obeying them.*

Idea

If you don't already read the Bible regularly, why not start now ? Get hold of a version you understand, and a guide or some notes to help you. Ask your minister or group leader for ideas.

What's the

LOAD

The group were having a crisis talk. Just before the meeting the vicar had phoned Anna with bad news. The council had decided to pull down the old hall they met in, and there would be nowhere for the youth club to meet. What could they do?

Well, they could pray. Everyone agreed that. But what should they pray?

Sandra said it was obvious...they should pray for the council to change their minds. Tariq said it was a bit late for that, 'cos it's not fair to go running to God and ask him to do miracles. He's not a magician. They ought to have been praying months ago so they didn't make the decision in the first place.

Nigel agreed, but he said they could pray for a new place to meet. And they probably ought to pray for the councillors too,

that God would forgive them.

Mike took a different line. 'What's the use of praying?' he said. 'It's just wishful thinking. Better to get on and do something practical.'

'Like what?'

'Well, we could make a petition....'

'If that's the best we can do we are a hopeless lot,' said Sandra. 'Why don't we just get on and pray?'

So they did. They all sat round in a circle and closed their eyes. Nobody said anything. After a few minutes somebody giggled. One by one they opened their eyes and looked at each other. Were they doing it right? Had God heard them? Would it change anything? Or were they just conning themselves?

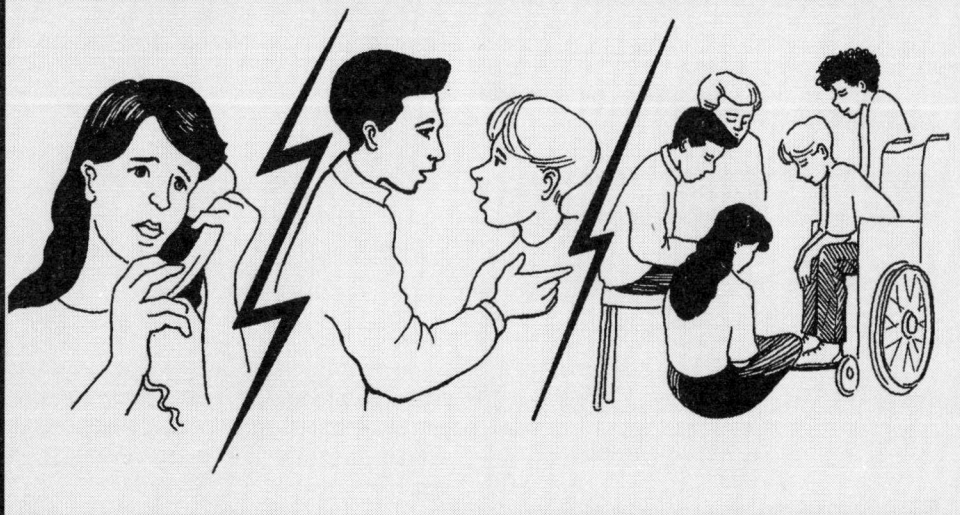

use of praying ?

 What do you think the group should do? What should they pray for?

 Put a ring round the answer that describes your experience of prayer.

A = always
S = sometimes
N = never

I pray....

....kneeling down	A	S	N
....out loud	A	S	N
....with members of my family	A	S	N
....in a crisis	A	S	N
....for my own needs	A	S	N
....when I feel close to God	A	S	N
....even when I don't feel like it	A	S	N

When I pray....

....I feel stupid	A	S	N
....I use special words	A	S	N
....I feel close to God	A	S	N
....God answers my prayers	A	S	N
....God gives me what I want	A	S	N

Compare your experience of prayer with one or two others in the group. What things do you have in common? Are there any ways you could help each other?

Which of these pictures comes closest to the way you think about prayer? Tick one or think of your own picture.

Getting on the hot line to the President ❑
Crossing your fingers and hoping for
   the best ❑
Talking to someone who really cares ❑
Falling for a con trick ❑
Telling someone you love them ❑
Waving a magic wand ❑
Asking a friend for a favour ❑

Other..

Explain your answer to the group.

Think of one time when you prayed and you are sure God heard you. What happened?

....

....

Now think of one time when you prayed and nothing seemed to happen. How did it feel? Why do you think it happened?

....

....

Share your experience with the group, if you want to.

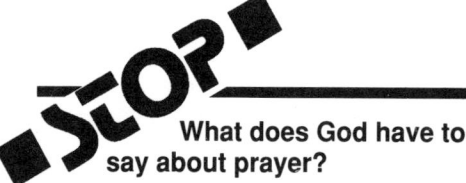

STOP
What does God have to say about prayer?

- Read the Bible passage.
- Mark any discoveries you make.
- Jot down any questions you are left with.
- Talk about your discoveries and questions with the group.....

What is Jesus' top priority in prayer?

PLAY
Here's some advice from Jesus on where, when and how to pray.

Is it OK to pray in a group?
What point is Jesus making here?

What kind of prayers does God like best?

'WHEN you pray, do not be like the hypocrites! They love to stand up and pray in the houses of worship and on the street corners, so that everyone will see them. I assure you, they have already been paid in full. But when you pray, go to your room, close the door, and pray to your Father, who is unseen. And your Father, who sees what you do in private, will reward you.

'When you pray, do not use a lot of meaningless words, as the pagans do, who think that God will hear them because their prayers are long. Do not be like them. Your Father already knows what you need before you ask him. This, then, is how you should pray:

What does this mean?

"Our Father in heaven:
    May your holy name be
        honoured;
    may your Kingdom come;
    may your will be done on earth
        as it is in heaven.
    Give us today the food we
        need.
    Forgive us the wrongs we have
        done,
    as we forgive the wrongs that
        others have done to us.
    Do not bring us to hard testing,
        but keep us safe from the
        Evil One.'"

Matthew 6:5–13

Does this just mean food?
What's the point in asking
God for food unless you live
in a country where people
are starving?

Are we allowed to ask God
to give us things? If so what?

FAST FORWARD

Look at these statements. Are they true or false – or is it hard to say?

 Ring: T for true
F for false
M for maybe.

You have to use special words to pray	T	F	M
You shouldn't pray standing up	T	F	M
Short prayers are good	T	F	M
You mustn't ask God for things	T	F	M
God always hears prayers	T	F	M

 What are your priorities in prayer? Number these types of prayer from 1–5 according to how important they are in your prayers. (1 = most important, 5 = least important.)

Asking for things from God	.....	.....
Praising God	.....	.....
Asking God to protect you	.....	.....
Asking for forgiveness	.....	.....
Offering your life to God	.....	.....

Now in the other column, write down the priorities Jesus had in the model prayer you have just read.

 If God knows everything we need, why doesn't he give it to us anyway? Why does he wait for us to pray?

 Look through this prayer together. Whoever prayed it has some pretty funny ideas about prayer!

Most gracious, merciful and bountiful heavenly Father,

This is just a quickee to remind thee about my French test today. It's about time you let me come top. After all, I am a pretty good Christian, so do your best.

God bless Uncle George.

Oh, and thanks for the shirt Mum got me, only please help her next time 'cos she's got such terrible taste.

You remember that argument I had with her about not doing the washing up yesterday? Well please make her less bad tempered. Forgive her for being wrong. Make her see that I shouldn't have to do it.

And please help the starving millions in Africa. Make them patient, 'cos the two quid I gave should be getting there soon.

Must dash.
Amen.

Mark the things that show that this person has not understood about prayer.

 Why is prayer important in your life? (Tick one or more.)

It gives me access to God's power	❑
It helps me to cope with life's problems	❑
It helps to pass the time	❑
It keeps me in touch with God	❑
It acts as a safety valve – I can tell God everything	❑
It isn't important	❑
Other..	

Explain your answer to the group.

WHAT WILL YOU DO?

You have been praying for a girl you know who has cancer. Your friends know you are praying for her, but instead of getting better she seems to be getting worse. What will you do?

TOUGH TALKING

Why do some prayers seem to go unanswered?

If God answers person A's prayer but doesn't seem to answer person B's prayer, does it mean that B's life is not as good as A's?

GOING FURTHER

If you want to think more about prayer, check out these Bible passages :

Luke 11:5–13 – Ask and you will receive
James 5:7–18 – Prayer at work
Psalm 16 – Praying and trusting

||PAUSE||

This outline for prayer is based on Jesus' prayer. Fill in some or all of the gaps, then use it for your own prayer, or share it with another member of the group.

Father God,
I praise you because ....

....

You know I need ....

....

Please forgive me for ....

....

Please protect me from ....
Amen.

Idea
Ask each member of the group to share one thing that they would like the rest of the group to pray about. Write them down in this book.

Either agree to pray for each other during the week, or agree a time when you will all pray about each other's requests.

Make sure there is time when you next meet to share what happened!

Ideas for

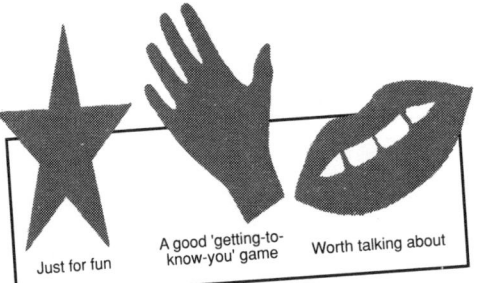

Just for fun   A good 'getting-to-know-you' game   Worth talking about

Who are you ?

This is a getting-to-know-you game. Everyone finds a partner, preferably someone they don't know too well. Person A asks person B, 'Who are you ?' Person B should answer with their name. Then person A asks again, 'Who are you ?' Person B should give another piece of information, eg, 'I'm Sarah's brother.' Then person A asks again, and gets another piece of information, eg, 'I'm a member of Windleston School choir.' Go on till person A has asked, 'Who are you ?' five times, then swap over.

When you've both had a go, each person introduces their partner to the rest of the group using the information they've collected....'This is Ben, he's Sarah's brother, he's a member of Windleston school choir....' and so on.

Musical laps

One person controls the music. The rest of the group stands in a circle, all facing the same way (ie clockwise or anti-clockwise). Hold onto the waist of the person in front of you. When you've finished tickling each other you can get on with the game!

You need to stand squeezed up as tight as you can together. While the music plays, you walk or shuffle around in a circle (which does need to be a round circle!) When the music stops everyone immediately sits down on the knees of the person behind. If you all stay up in the sitting position, supporting yourselves on each others' knees, you've won. If some or all of you fall to the floor, you've all lost.

If your group manages to do it and you're feeling pretty confident, then while you are all supporting each other try extending both arms out level with your shoulders. If you still haven't collapsed, shuffle around, in the sitting position, in time with the music.

To win at this game, everyone involved has to work together to keep the circle up. If one goes, you all go....

People to people

You need an odd number of people to play this game. In fact, the odder the better! Get into pairs. The extra person starts off as caller. She or he gives instructions which everybody must follow. You must put your bodies into the positions that the caller says. For instance, you may want to start off with simple instructions like 'Hand to hand' or 'Feet to feet', (or even 'Lips to lips'!) Work your way up to more complicated instructions like 'Foot to head' – both of you put a foot to your partner's head – or 'Heels to heels and nose to nose.' After a few calls the caller says 'People to people', at which point everyone grabs a new partner. The caller should make sure that she or he gets a partner and the new person left over becomes the caller.

Keep going, changing callers until everyone who wants to has had a go at calling. Be as imaginative as possible but try to stay within the limits of decency and physical possibility!

Word famine

A word famine has struck the land. There are not enough words to go round. Words

your group

are rationed to just four each. Give each group member a pencil and paper, then take a couple of minutes for each person to choose just four words. When you've chosen your four words, join up in pairs and try to communicate. You can only use the four words you have chosen, plus gestures.

When you've tried this, share your words with your partner. Now you have eight words to communicate with. See how you get on. Then choose another partner and share their words too, so that there are sixteen on your list. Have another go at communicating. Finally, choose one last partner and share their words so that you have thirty-two words.

If there is time, see if you can use your thirty-two words to write a poem or make a prayer.

Egg grenades

This is an outdoor game. Two people stand facing each other at arm's length. One person has an egg grenade (ie a fresh egg) which is timed to explode any minute. He passes it to the other person. They both then take a step back, and the egg is passed or thrown gently back to the first person. They take another step back, and so on. Keep on throwing and catching until disaster strikes! If you don't want to use an egg, try using a water-filled balloon. The effect is similar. Make sure that everyone who wants to can have a go.

One word stories

All sit in a circle. You are going to make up a story together. One person is chosen to start. He or she says 'Once'. The person on their right adds 'upon'. The person on their right adds 'a', and the person on their

right adds 'time'. Then the story continues round the circle. Each person adds one word, and the story unfolds by itself. Some amazing stories have been made up this way. The only problem is deciding when to stop!

Be our guest !

It's easy to get tired of the same old faces! But it's good to welcome new faces to the group, especially if they get the chance to share the fun and hear the good news about Jesus.

Once in a while, why not set aside a special time to invite guests to join the group? You could invite people from school or work, or people who live nearby. Perhaps you could make or print some special invitation cards too. You could meet in someone's home, or organise a special outing.

Think carefully about how you can make your guests welcome. They may not enjoy singing a lot of choruses they don't know. But a few good games could break the ice. It may be right to have a talk or discussion about what it means to be a Christian. You could work through a track from this book together, or show a video, or just have a fun evening together. How about a pancake party or a treasure hunt or a crisp tasting contest ? Plan well and make it a fun event, so that everyone feels they want to come again.

What about

LOAD

The Youth Club had decided to branch out. It was too easy, they thought, to meet every Sunday night and talk about God and sing and have a good time together. It was time they started challenging some other people to come. After all, there must be dozens of young people around who didn't know about God. Hundreds even. So they sent Karen off to make a poster for the library.

When Karen saw the notice board her eyes nearly popped out of her head. There must have been fifty posters on the one small board. They were all on top of each other, and some were hanging on by one drawing pin. There were posters for yoga classes, political meetings, an Asian interest group, one about animal rights, and something called Tai Chi. There was a poster for the Revelation Church, but it was half covered by something about The Voice of the Prophet. Suddenly her poster seemed very small and a bit silly. So many people believing so many different things. How could they all be so sure they were right ?

A man came and put up a poster in the middle of the board. It was about a meet-ing being held by a group called The New Way. It said the speaker would 'tell the truth about God you've never heard before.'

'Excuse me,' said Karen, 'but is The New Way a Christian group ?'

'Oh yes,' said the man. 'In fact we're the only really Christian group. For all these years the churches have been missing the truth about Jesus, but we've found it.'

'How can you be so sure ?'

'God has shown it to us. And he'll show it to you too if you want. Why not come along to the meeting on Sunday evening ? There's no charge.'

What do you think Karen should do? (Tick one or more or add your own answers.)

Go along to the meeting to see what it's about ❏

Put up her poster and pray that people see it ❏

Avoid talking to strange men ❏
Invite the man to the youth group ❏
Work harder at understanding her own religion ❏
Take down all the other posters ❏

Other ....

other gods ?

When I meet a person whose religious beliefs are different from mine, I tend to feel....

more ——————————————— *less*
.... sure about my own faith.

(Mark the line with an **✗**.)

When I meet people who hold beliefs different from mine they tend to be....

more ——————————————— *less*
.... committed to their faith than I am to mine.

In what ways is Christianity different from any other religion or belief you know about? (Tick one or more.)

It talks about God ❏
It tells people how they can get to
    heaven ❏
It says that Jesus was both God and
    a real human being ❏
It's the oldest religion in the world ❏
It says that anyone can get to heaven
    if they're good enough ❏
It says that God has visited the earth ❏
It's the only truly British religion ❏

Other..

How strongly do you agree or disagree with the following statements? Put a ring round your answer.

SA = strongly agree
TA = tend to agree
TD = tend to disagree
SD = strongly disagree

There is only one real God
  SA   TA   TD   SD

All religions are partly true
  SA   TA   TD   SD

People should stick to the religion they are brought up with
  SA   TA   TD   SD

It doesn't matter what you believe as long as you believe it strongly
  SA   TA   TD   SD

People who don't believe in Jesus will go to hell
  SA   TA   TD   SD

Do you think The New Way is a Christian group? What makes you think it is or isn't ?

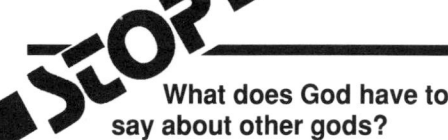

What does God have to say about other gods?

- Read the Bible passage.
- Mark any discoveries you make.
- Jot down any questions you are left with.
- Talk about your discoveries and questions with the group.....

PLAY

In Athens there were many temples with statues of Greek gods. They even had a spare one in case they'd left a god out! Paul told the people there was only one true God. The book of Acts tells us that 'Paul was preaching about Jesus and the resurrection.'

Why was Paul so upset?

Was Paul being sarcastic?

WHILE Paul was waiting in Athens for Silas and Timothy he was greatly upset when he noticed how full of idols the city was. So he held discussions in the synagogue with the Jews and with the Gentiles who worshipped God, and also in the public square every day with the people who happened to pass by....

Paul stood up in front of the city council and said, 'I see that in every way you Athenians are very religious. For as I walked through your city and looked at the places where you worship, I found an altar on which is written, "To an Unknown God." That which you worship, then, even though you do not know it, is what I now

What is special about
the true God, according to Paul?

> idol, n. Describes anything
> that has been made by a human
> being and is worshipped like a
> god.

proclaim to you. God, who made the world and everything in it, is Lord of heaven and earth and does not live in man-made temples. Nor does he need any-thing that we can supply by working for him, since it is he himself who gives life and breath and everything else to everyone. From one man he created all races of mankind and made them live throughout the whole earth. He himself fixed beforehand the exact times and the limits of the places where they would live. He did this so that they would look for him, and perhaps find him as they felt about for him. Yet God is actually not far from any one of us; as someone has said, "In him we live and move and exist." '

Acts 17:16–17, 22–28a

Is the true God only interested
in some people, or in everyone?

▶ PLAY

How do people 'feel about' for God?
Where did Paul say we can find
the true God?

FAST FORWARD

TWOS Which of these sentences describes Paul's message to the people in Athens? (Tick one or more.)

You stick to your gods and I'll stick to mine ❏

If you don't know Jesus you don't know God yet ❏

I've discovered a new god you might like to hear about ❏

You're so close to the truth you could almost touch it ❏

There are so many real gods it must be hard to choose ❏

The God who made the world is the only true god ❏

TWOS Following Paul's example, what should our attitude be to people with other beliefs about God? (Put an X on the line somewhere between the two extremes.)

Listen and _____ Don't let
learn   them get
                                            a word in

Tell them _____ Avoid
about Jesus   them
                                            altogether

Treat them _____ Treat as
as friends   them as
                                            enemies

GROUP Why do you think Paul concentrated on telling people about Jesus?

SOLO How well do you think you know God? (Mark an X on the line.)
Very well _____ Not at all

How well do you think God knows you? (Mark an X on the line.)
Very well _____ Not at all

SOLO Write down one thing you could do in the coming weeks to help you to get to know God better.

....

....

SOLO God knows us, and he knows all our needs. But what about this group? How many marks out of ten would you give them for....

Knowing you .....
Trusting you .....
Listening to you .....
Understanding you .....
Caring for you .....
Making you feel you belong .....

Share your scores with the group.

||PAUSE||

WHAT WILL YOU DO?

Two people come to your house offering to sell you a magazine. They say the proceeds of the sale will go to 'missionary work'. You chat to them for ten minutes. They say they are Christians, and they do seem to know their Bibles well. They invite you to a meeting at the weekend. What will you do?

 GROUP Pray together or in silence for....

....the millions of people who don't know the true God
....people who work to spread the good news about Jesus
....people you know from other faiths and cultures

To finish, stand in a circle, holding hands if you wish, and say the grace together, looking round at each other.

May the grace of our Lord Jesus Christ, the love of God and the fellowship of the Holy Spirit be with us all, evermore. Amen.

Then greet each other with a handshake or a hug.

TOUGH TALKING

Should Christians meet with people of other faiths to try to understand their beliefs ? Can Christians learn anything about God from members of other religions?

If people of other religions live in Britain should they be expected to adopt traditional British ways of life?

GOING FURTHER

If you want to think more about other gods check out the following Bible passages :

Psalm 115 — The one true God

Isaiah 44:9–20 — Idols are stupid

2 John 1–13 — False teachers

What can I

LOAD

Carmel always seems too busy for church activities. No matter what you want her to do, whether it's to sing in the worship group or deliver leaflets for a special service, she always has something else to do.

She's always making tea for her sisters because her mum's at work, or off to visit her gran, or she has a friend coming round for a chat; and then she's on the school charity committee so there's a teacher kidnap or a sponsored jelly-suck to organise. Never mind that there's something important on in the church, like a praise procession, or a Bible study, or an evangelistic meeting of the flower-arranging club. Once she missed a prayer meeting because she'd promised her friends she'd go to the disco. 'Well!' thought everybody at the Youth Fellowship. 'What sort of a witness is that when all her friends know she's a Christian?'

Of course she's at church most Sundays, but, as her church friends tell her, 'It's not enough to be a Sunday Christian! If you don't make time for God, how can you be sure he'll make time for you? Get your priorities right, Carmel!' But she just smiles and says, 'Why don't you come round for a coffee some time? Or better still, come to tea!'

SOLO Fill in the bubbles to show what you think these people think of Carmel:

eg Church friends

She's not a good Christian. She doesn't make time to do things for God.

Her mum

Her gran

School friends

do for God ?

Draw yourself, and fill in what *you* think of Carmel and the way she spends her time.

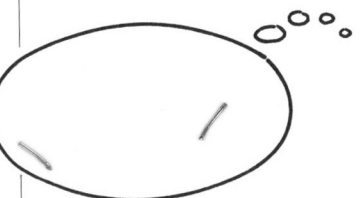

Show each other how you have filled in the bubbles. Decide together how pleased you think God is with the way that Carmel and her church friends spend their time.

Mark an **X** somewhere on each line to show how pleased or sad he is with :

Carmel:
Very pleased ———————— *Very sad*

Her friends at church:
Very pleased ———————— *Very sad*

Do you think Carmel has got her priorities right ? What about her friends? Why?

There are lots of things we can do for God and lots of ways to serve him. Here are some ideas. Which ones would you find easy to do, and which ones would you find hard? Add your own ideas.

DE = dead easy
FE = fairly easy
QH = quite hard
VH = very hard

Helping to lead worship
DE   FE   QH   VH

Helping at home
DE   FE   QH   VH

Visiting an elderly person
DE   FE   QH   VH

Raising money for charity
DE   FE   QH   VH

Cleaning the church
DE   FE   QH   VH

Scrubbing bad graffiti off walls
DE   FE   QH   VH

Working in the Third World
DE   FE   QH   VH

Babysitting for a single parent
DE   FE   QH   VH

Telling friends about Jesus
DE   FE   QH   VH

Cleaning up a dirty river-bed
DE   FE   QH   VH

Befriending a lonely person
DE   FE   QH   VH

Other..
DE   FE   QH   VH

Other..
DE   FE   QH   VH

STOP

What does God have to say about how to serve him?

- Read the Bible passages.
- Mark any discoveries you make.
- Jot down any questions you are left with.
- Talk about your discoveries and questions with the group.....

What sort of people are hungry or homeless today? Are there other sorts of 'hunger' apart from lack of food?

PLAY

When the prophet Isaiah was alive lots of people prayed and fasted and worshipped God, but at the same time they treated poor people very badly. God sent a message through Isaiah saying this was not good enough.

Will God only be with us if we do the things mentioned here?

'THE kind of fasting I want is this: Remove the chains of oppression and the yoke of injustice, and let the oppressed go free. Share your food with the hungry and open your homes to the homeless poor. Give clothes to those who have nothing to wear, and do not refuse to help your own relatives.

'Then my favour will shine on you like the morning sun, and your wounds will be quickly healed. I will always be with you to save you; my presence will protect you on every side. When you pray, I will answer you. When you call to me, I will respond.'

Isaiah 58:6–9a

Matthew describes how Jesus spent his time, and how he told his disciples to spend theirs.

Fasting means going without food or other important things. It is a way of concentrating on God and showing him that you want to serve him. People also fast sometimes when they want God to do something important.

JESUS went round visiting all the towns and villages. He taught in the synagogues, preached the Good News about the Kingdom, and healed people with every kind of disease and sickness. As he saw the crowds, his heart was filled with pity for them, because they were worried and helpless, like sheep without a shepherd. So he said to his disciples, 'The harvest is large, but there are few workers to gather it in. Pray to the owner of the harvest that he will send out workers to gather in his harvest.'

Jesus called his twelve disciples together and gave them authority to drive out evil spirits and to heal every disease and every sickness.

Matthew 9:35–10:1

who or what is the owner of the harvest?

Jesus used this picture because he was in a farming community. What picture might he have used to describe people in our area?

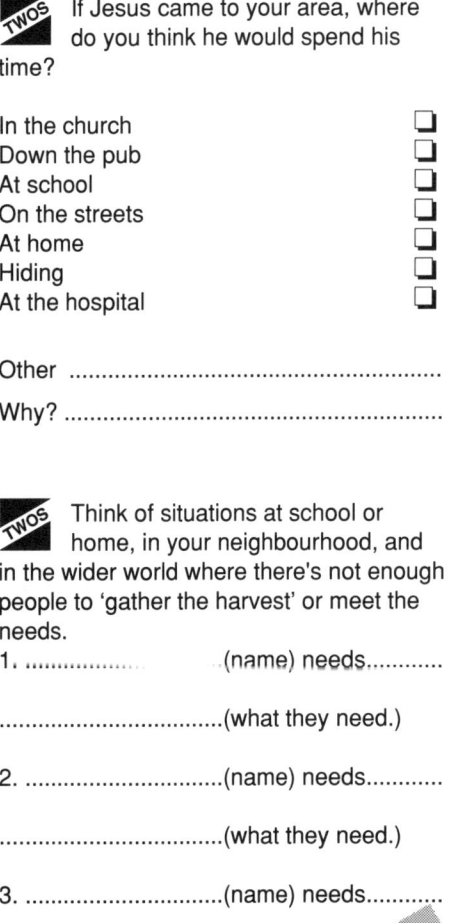

FASE FORWARD

TWOS Try to imagine what it was like to gather in a harvest in Jesus' time, before the invention of modern machinery. In what ways is serving God like bringing in a harvest? Share your ideas with the group.

TWOS If Jesus came to your area, where do you think he would spend his time?

In the church ❏
Down the pub ❏
At school ❏
On the streets ❏
At home ❏
Hiding ❏
At the hospital ❏

Other ....

Why? ....

TWOS Think of situations at school or home, in your neighbourhood, and in the wider world where there's not enough people to 'gather the harvest' or meet the needs.

1. .... (name) needs............

..............................(what they need.)

2. ....(name) needs............

..............................(what they need.)

3. ....(name) needs............

..............................(what they need.)

GROUP Where could you see a crowd of worried and helpless people today?

SOLO In the left hand column, list all the members of this group. Then in the right hand column choose one special gift or talent that God has given them that could be used to serve him. Perhaps it's something they already do. Or it could be something you think they would be good at. Look back at the list of ways people can serve God (in the LOAD section) or use your own ideas.

Then go round to everyone in the group in turn. Tell them what you've put down for them, and find out what they've put down for you.

Name	Ways she/he could serve God
eg Jackie	Caring for sick people
....	....
....	....
....	....
....	....
....	....
....	....
....	....
....	....
....	....

WHAT WILL YOU DO?

You've been telling one of your friends about Jesus, and she even agreed to come to church with you once. Now she has asked you to go with her to see a film she really wants to see. But the only time she can go is Sunday evening when you usually go to church. What will you do?

TOUGH TALKING

Can people who don't claim to be Christians still do things that please God and help to build his kingdom?

If God wants you to do something but you don't do it, does it remain undone, or will he get someone else to do it?

GOING FURTHER

If you want to think more about serving God, check out these Bible passages :

Romans 12:1–21 – *Life in God's service*
Acts 6:1–7 – *An example of serving*
Matthew 25:31–46 – *Serve God by serving others*

||PAUSE||

Ask each person in the group to mention one of the needs they have written down on page 28. Then choose at least three that individuals or the group as a whole can do something about. You might decide to pray, write a letter, raise some money or go and do something practical. Note the three situations on the action sheet, and decide who is going to act on them.

Action sheet
(1) Situation..........................
needs................................
Action...............................
Person/people ....
(2) Situation ....
needs................................
Action...............................
Person/people ....
(3) Situation.........................
needs................................
Action...............................
Person/people ....

Now pray together about the action you're going to take to serve God this week.

❝ Lance Pierson says, when you meet to look at the Bible....

Don't leave God out of it!

It's a very odd family where no one ever talks to Dad or elder brother, even when they're in the room. And it's a very odd group that meets to look at the Bible and hear what God has to say, but never speaks to him. That's why it's good to spend time focussing on God whenever you meet as a group. You are his family; he's there with you.

So every track in these books has a PAUSE section. It's a chance to stop and talk to God about the things you've been thinking about together. And I don't mean just saying hello. You can have a real conversation. God speaks to you, and you answer him in your prayers.

But in case you want to do something different from what it says in the PAUSE section – or perhaps do something else on top – here are a few suggestions. You could take them as they are, or change them to fit into the subject you've been looking at. **❞**

•SILENCE•

God can hear your silent words and thoughts just as well as the ones you speak out loud.

1 Praying for one another One way to make sure everyone is prayed for is for each person to pray silently for the people sitting next to them – one on the left and one on the right.

2 Meditating This simply means thinking more deeply about something in God's presence. One way is for everyone to write down their full address (including continent, planet, planetary system, galaxy, universe!). Then slowly and silently read it in reverse order, remembering God's love and concern for every place you come to. Finally remember his love and concern for you.

•SPOKEN PRAYER•

'Extemporary' prayer (where you make up your own prayer as you go along) is not the only kind that God enjoys. Here are two other ways.

1 Written prayers Everyone writes a short prayer to be read in the prayer time. You could give different people different subjects to pray about. And perhaps you could ask everyone to give their prayer to someone else to read.

2 Set words There are other prayers we can say together, apart from 'The Grace' or 'The Lord's Prayer'. You could say the prayer of St Francis ('Lord, make me a channel of your peace') or other prayer-songs in the hymn-book which are sometimes good to say. Or you could get a book of prayers or meditations for one person to read out.

•ACTION•

God doesn't only want us to say we love him, but to show it in action.

1 Offerings It is sometimes good to have a collection of money (like in church!) for a special appeal. Or you can put written promises of money, time or 'New Year resolutions' (at any time of year) into a box or bag, so that only God sees them.

2 Do something positive When God speaks to us he often asks us to do something; to go on serving him and responding to him after the meeting.
    If there's a practical project or need to be met, why not get together and do it as a group?

•MUSIC•

Lots of groups are put off singing because they don't have anyone who plays the guitar or piano. But why not give it a try without ? Never mind if your music teacher always told you you were tone deaf – just find a note and sing.

So how about.....

1 Sing all the way through (on and off!) Pause in the middle of the track to sing something that comes to mind, or that echoes the Bible words. Or mix some songs of praise and love into your prayer time; it can help to keep your mind fixed on God. Make sure you choose ones that everyone's familiar with.

2 Mix prayer into the songs During or after a suitable song, ask a musician to keep playing quietly in the background while other people take turns to pray one word or one sentence on the same theme....eg things to thank God for; names of people who need prayer; names of Jesus (Saviour, Lord, Good Shepherd, etc).

WHY NOT?

◆ ...use these pages to help you think about worship in your group.

◆ ...talk together about what helps you to worship God, and what puts you off.

◆ ...try something you've never done before, using Lance's suggestions.

Am I ready to pass

LOAD

We were all stood on the touchline watching the fifth form team get hammered by Winton Park. Lenny was leading the cheering – not that there was much to cheer about. Two – nil down with three minutes to play. Suddenly Mike was left with a clear run at the goal. 'Shoot, for God's sake!' shouted Lenny. He did. The keeper dived the wrong way, but Mike's shot swerved and clipped the outside of the post. The whistle blew and the match was lost.

'Jesus Christ!' said Lenny, turning away disgusted.

'Don't say that,' said Carol, grinning at Lenny. 'You'll upset Simon. He's in the God squad.'

'He can't be,' said Lenny scornfully. 'He's got more sense.'

'He is.' said Carol. 'You ask him.'

I'd been dreading that. What on earth would I say? I mean you can hardly tell your friends you're a Christian, can you? Not if you want to keep them. A person

like Lenny would never stop laughing. Perhaps I should deny it. He turned to me.

'Well, is it true? Do you believe in God?'

I decided to take the plunge. 'Well, yeah.'

'I suppose you go to church then do you?'

'Well, er...'

'So what difference does it make, being a Christian?'

It was then I noticed that Lenny wasn't laughing. He seemed really interested. As we walked home he asked me a load of questions about being a Christian. I couldn't answer all of them. But at least he took me seriously.

Jesus Christ!

TWOS Choose a word (or invent one) to describe how Simon felt when he thought Lenny was going to ask him about Jesus.

....

Choose a word to describe how he felt when he got home.

....

SOLO How would you feel if someone asked you questions about being a Christian? (Mark an ✗ on the line to indicate your answer.)

Embarrassed ——————————Pleased

Confident ——————————— Scared

Ready to ———————————Unprepared
answer

the message on ?

GROUP Here is a list of some of the ways that people first hear about Jesus. Put a tick beside any that apply to you.

I was brought up in a Christian home ☐
Someone invited me to church ☐
I read a Christian book ☐
A friend spoke to me about Jesus ☐
Someone I didn't know spoke to me
    about Jesus ☐
I went to a Christian meeting ☐
I felt God was speaking to me ☐

Other ....

Now add up the scores from the whole group and see which of these ways were most important in your group's experience.

TWOS Think back to the last time you talked about Jesus with someone who was not a Christian. Complete these sentences, and then use them to tell your story to your partner. (If you have never talked to anyone about Jesus, you might like to tell your partner about the last time someone spoke to you about Jesus.)

The last time I spoke to someone about Jesus was

....

The person I spoke to was

....

The opportunity arose because

....

The result was

....

TWOS What would you have said if you had been asked the same questions as Simon? How would you have answered? Think of the first few words of your answer.

Do you believe in God?

I suppose you go to church then do you?

What difference does it make, being a Christian?

GROUP Have you ever had to decide whether to talk about your faith or keep quiet? What did you do? What happened? What did you learn from it? Tell the group about it.

What did Jesus tell his disciples to do? How do you think they felt when they got their instructions?

STOP

What does God have to say about passing the message on?

■ Read the Bible passages.
■ Mark any discoveries you make.
■ Jot down any questions you are left with.
■ Talk about your discoveries and questions with the group.....

PLAY

Just before Jesus left the earth he met with his disciples to give them some final instructions.

JESUS drew near and said to them, 'I have been given all authority in heaven and on earth. Go, then, to all peoples everywhere and make them my disciples: baptize them in the name of the Father, the Son, and the Holy Spirit, and teach them to obey everything I have commanded you. And I will be with you always, to the end of the age.'

Matthew 28:18–20

How could he be with them if he was just going away?

What does an ambassador do?

What is a disciple?
How do you make someone
a disciple?

In his second letter to them, Paul told the
Christians in Corinth why it was important
for them to pass the message on.

W HEN someone becomes a
Christian he becomes a
brand new person inside. He is
not the same any more. A new
life has begun!

All these new things are from
God, who brought us back to
himself through what Christ
Jesus did. And God has given us
the privilege of urging everyone
to come into his favour and be
reconciled to him. For God was
in Christ, restoring the world to
himself, no longer counting
men's sins against them but blot-
ting them out. This is the won-
derful message he has given us
to tell others. We are Christ's
ambassadors. God is using us to
speak to you: we beg you, as
though Christ himself were here
pleading with you, receive the
love he offers you – be reconciled to God.

2 Corinthians 5:17-20
(Living Bible)

What happens when someone
becomes a Christian? What
changed when you became
a Christian?

What are the main
points of the message God
has given us?

FAST FORWARD

TWOS Why should we pass on the good news about Jesus? Tick the three reasons you think are most important.

So that people will agree with what we believe ❏

So that we will get new members for this group ❏

So that people will know God loves them ❏

Because Jesus told us to ❏

So that people won't go to hell ❏

So that people can be reconciled to God ❏

So that God will see what good Christians we are ❏

So that people can have their sins blotted out ❏

Other...

TWOS What do you think you need to do to be a good ambassador for Christ ? Tick any answers you agree with, or add your own.

Learn how to explain the good news about Jesus ❏

Tell your friends when they are doing wrong things ❏

Be friendly to people ❏

Only mix with Christians ❏

Go to Bible college ❏

Make opportunities to tell people about Jesus ❏

Write Bible verses on the school walls ❏

Argue with teachers who are not Christians ❏

Talk about Jesus whenever you can ❏

Other ....

Other ....

GROUP Write an anonymous message to each member of the group saying 'thank you' for their contribution to the group. Try to say a few words that you think will be a particular encouragement to them. You could write out one of the 'good news' messages from God that are printed here, or you could add a few words of your own.

When you've written your message to each person in the group 'post' them in a box.

■ Jesus said : 'I will never turn away anyone who comes to me' *(John 6:37)*.

■ 'Christ is in you, which means that you will share in the glory of God' *(Colossians 1:27)*.

■ Jesus said : 'I will be with you always, to the end of the age' *(Matthew 28:20)*.

■ 'The LORD's unfailing love and mercy still continue, fresh as the morning, as sure as the sunrise' *(Lamentations 3:22,23)*.

■ 'Tears may flow in the night but, joy comes in the morning' *(Psalm 30:5)*.

TWOS Jesus said to his disciples, 'You will be my witnesses in Jerusalem, and in Judea and all Samaria, and to the ends of the earth.'

Fill in the places where Jesus wants you to be a witness for him.

You will be my witnesses in ....

and in .... and to the ends of the earth.

GROUP How could this group work together to pass on the good news about Jesus? (See the item 'Be our guest!' on page 17.)

WHAT WILL YOU DO?

On Saturday night you went to a Christian concert and on Sunday morning you went to church. On Monday morning your non-Christian friends are talking about how they spent the weekend. What will you do?

TOUGH TALKING

Are there some people who will never become Christians because God has decided they won't? What will happen to people who never get the chance to hear about Jesus?

Is it better to tell people that you are a Christian, or to keep quiet and show it by the way you behave?

‖PAUSE‖

GROUP Many Christians meet regulary in prayer triplets to pray for their friends. The idea is that three people agree to meet together, and each of them thinks of three friends who are not Christians. The triplet agrees to pray regularly for all nine people to get to know and follow Jesus.

Divide into threes now and mention the names of three people who don't yet know Jesus. They could be friends, work-mates or members of your family. Then pray for these people, and ask God to give you opportunities to speak to them about Jesus.

Decide whether you would like to go on meeting regularly in your triplet.

GOING FURTHER

If you want to think more about passing the message on, check out these Bible passages :

Ezekiel 3:1–11, 16–21

 – Ezekiel's responsibility

Matthew 10:26–33

 – Don't be afraid to speak

Acts 8:26–40

 – Philip's example

What's my

LOAD

The service ended and everyone trooped out into the winter night, their breath hanging on the air in clouds.

Mark looked frustrated. 'That service left me completely cold,' he said to Sue. 'How anyone can feel close to God in a church with no central heating and a hymn-book written in the Stone Age beats me.'

'It's not all about feelings you know,' said Sue. 'God's there whether you feel it or not.'

'I wish I could be so sure.'

Sue and Mark stood hand in hand at the edge of the recreation ground. Although the rec was covered in snow, Sue felt warm and content. They huddled together, staring up into the night sky. Constellations and stars and planets glimmered brightly against the dark winter night.

'This is where I feel close to God,' said Mark. 'Don't you sense it? He feels so close when you look at all this. Just think, here we are, standing on the edge of one star, and out there somewhere, I know he's smiling at us. You don't think it's stupid to feel like this do you?'

God like?

 If you were Sue, how would you answer Mark's question?

 How do you picture God? Look at each of these pairs and circle the one that comes closest to your picture of God. There are no right answers, so use your imagination!

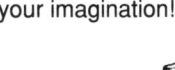

A lion   A pet dog

A policeman   A nurse

A businessman   A beggar

A motorbike   A rowing boat

A mother   A father

Now ask each person in the group to explain one of the five choices he or she made.

 When I think about God I feel....

close • God who? • angry • let down

distant • best friends • mixed-up

great • excited • bored • happy • afraid

interested • peaceful • uncertain

Ring one or more words or add your own.

 'It's not all about feelings you know.'
What did Sue mean by this? Apart from our feelings, what other evidence do we have that God is there?

 In this group I feel....

cared for • trusted • I belong

close to God • understood • out of place

a stranger • comfortable • bored

Put a ring round the answers that best complete the sentence. Or you could think of your own ending for the sentence. Then share your answers with the group, if you want to.

Is God really like this, or was Isaiah dreaming?

■STOP■
What does God have to say about himself?

- ■ Read the Bible passages.
- ■ Mark any discoveries you make.
- ■ Jot down any questions you are left with.
- ■ Talk about your discoveries and questions with the group.....

What does 'holy' mean?

►PLAY►
In this passage the prophet Isaiah describes a surprise meeting with God, and how it made him feel.

Why did Isaiah react like this?

Iɴ the year that King Uzziah died, I saw the Lᴏʀᴅ. He was sitting on his throne, high and exalted, and his robe filled the whole Temple. Round him flaming creatures were standing, each of which had six wings. Each creature covered its face with two wings, and its body with two, and used the other two for flying. They were calling out to each other:

'Holy, holy, holy!
The Lᴏʀᴅ Almighty is holy!
His glory fills the world.'

The sound of their voices made the foundation of the Temple shake, and the Temple itself was filled with smoke.

I said, 'There is no hope for me! I am doomed because every word that passes my lips is sinful, and I live among a people whose every word is sinful. And yet, with my own eyes I have seen the King, the Lᴏʀᴅ Almighty!'

Isaiah 6:1–5

In what ways is God like a human king? In what ways is he not like a human king?

This passage from the Psalms is a lively hymn of praise.

S ING to the LORD, all the world!
  Worship the LORD with joy;
  come before him with happy
    songs!

How can we do this?

Acknowledge that the LORD is
    God.
  He made us, and we belong
    to him;
  we are his people, we are
    his flock.

temple, n. A huge building in Jerusalem. The Jews went there to worship God.

Enter the temple gates with
      thanks-giving,
  go into its courts with praise.
  Give thanks to him and praise
    him.

The LORD is good;
  his love is eternal
  and his faithfulness lasts
    for ever.

Psalm 100:1–5

Isaiah was afraid when he saw God, but this person was happy. Why?

FAST FORWARD

Look in the Bible passages for all the words that describe what God is like. Write them in the box.

GROUP

In comparison to Isaiah's story, my own meetings with God have been....

SOLO

Just as exciting ☐
More personal ☐
Rather tame ☐
Just as life-changing ☐
More intellectual ☐
Different, but just as real ☐

Other ....

What makes you feel specially close to God?
(Tick one or more)

TWOS

Seeing a beautiful sunset ☐
Being part of a big crowd ☐
Reading the Bible ☐
Listening to music ☐
Being in a group like this ☐
Seeing human bravery and self-sacrifice ☐
Being alone and quiet ☐
Going through pain or suffering ☐
Nothing – I've never felt close to God ☐

Other ....

Share your answers with the group.

Now you are coming to the end of this booklet, what could you do next as a group that will help you to....

GROUP

.... get to know God better?

....
....

.... know and care for each other more?

....
....

.... tell other people about Jesus?

....
....

||PAUSE||

WHAT WILL YOU DO?

A friend challenges you: 'Say what evidence you've got that God exists.' What will you do?

TOUGH TALKING

If God really is powerful and loving, why is there so much suffering in the world ? Why doesn't he stop it?

Do scientific discoveries about the way the world works make it more or less difficult to believe in God?

GOING FURTHER

If you want to think more about God, check out these Bible passages :

John 14:1–14 – Meet Jesus : meet God

1 John 4:7–18 – God is love

1 Kings 18:20–40 – God on trial

GROUP Sit in a circle and close your eyes. Keep silent for a minute or play some quiet music. Think together about God, and what he means to you. Think of some of the names by which God is known.

Anyone who wants to should quietly say one of the names of God – or a word that describes him. Each person could choose something about God that is important to them. The rest of the group respond by saying, 'God is with us now.' So for instance you may say :

God is my creator...
God is with us now;
God is a rock...
God is with us now;
God is forgiving...
God is with us now.

Here's a list of titles and qualities of God to get you going. You could glance through a Bible and find loads of others.

God is....
....my friend   ....my creator
....very powerful   ....my redeemer
....unchanging   ....my light
....holy   ....my shepherd
....always faithful   ....my Lord
....love   ....my provider
....king of kings   ....like a mother

How to use

This book has two aims....

■ **To help you hear what God has to say to you**
Of course there's no point in just hearing God speak for the sake of it. When God speaks to us he always wants us to change. So you need to decide how you will put what you hear into practice too.

■ **To help you grow together as a group**
The Christian life is for living together. That means getting to know each other, sharing ideas, encouraging each other and challenging each other to follow Jesus.

Here's how it works....

Each track in this book is divided into four sections :

LOAD This is the section to get you started. It's a chance for all the members of the group to share their ideas and experiences. Ask someone to read the scene-setter story aloud to the rest of the group. Then work through the questions that follow. You should work by yourselves, in pairs or all together as indicated by the symbols beside the questions. But try to work through the questions at the same pace so that no one gets left behind. Every member of your group is special. So make sure that everyone gets a chance to contribute.

PLAY The aim of this section is to find out what God has to say to you through his Word, the Bible.

You can either get together on this section or work individually. *Read through the Bible passages with a pencil in your hand. If anything strikes you as interesting, make a note of it in the book.* If there's anything you don't understand, or any questions you'd like answered, write them in too. We've pencilled in a few questions that occurred to us, but you can add your own.

When you've had a chance to work through the Bible passages and scribbled down your comments and questions, *get together with the rest of the group and talk through the questions you have raised, and the ones we thought of.* If there are too many questions to work through, choose the most important ones, or save some for another session. See if you can work out what God is saying through the Bible.

FAST FORWARD This is where the action starts. What are you going to do about the things that God is saying to you? Work through these questions as you did before. The *Fast forward* section always gives an opportunity for the members of the group to encourage and affirm one another, to share discoveries and to make plans.

What will you do? is a test of how much you have changed in the light of what you think God is saying. When it comes to the crunch what will you do? Decide for yourself then share your answer with the group. Be honest!

Tough talking is an optional section, mostly for older groups who like to struggle with hard questions. There are no easy answers here.

this book....

Going further is another optional section. It is not intended for you to use in the group session, but you may want to read through these passages in the week after the meeting to understand the subject even better. And they may help you with some of the *Tough talking* questions.

||PAUSE|| At the end of each track, take a *Pause* and spend some time focussing on God. Some groups will want to sing together or have a time of open prayer. If your group is not used to worship and praying together start with a few of the simpler ideas.

Making it work ...

Getting going

Every group meeting should start with a fun time to help everyone to relax together. This is particularly important if the members of the group don't know each other very well, or if there are new members. Ideas for breaking the ice are contained in the *Meeting points* section of the book. Pick on one or two of these ideas and enjoy them together. Don't be tempted to miss out this important warm-up stage of the group's meeting.

So much to do....so little time!

Different groups have different amounts of time available. Each track contains at least enough material for a whole evening together. Many groups won't be able to manage all the material at a single sitting. Don't worry! Either split the material over two or more sessions, or else select a couple of exercises from each section. It is much better to cover a few questions well than to try to do everything quickly. If one question seems particularly interesting or important for your group, spend longer on it. If there's a question that doesn't apply so much to you, just skip it.

Who's in charge?

Every group needs a leader. But it doesn't necessarily have to be the same person all the time. This book is designed so that group members could take it in turns to lead sessions. This is good experience, and it can also help to build the group if everyone agrees to co-operate with the session leader.

Here are some do's and don'ts for people leading a group session....

....do prepare!

Look through the material before the meeting. Decide what *Meeting points* you will use. Think about how long you want to spend on each section. Look carefully at the Bible passages and look up anything you think people may not understand. It may help if you have looked through the *Going further* passages too.

....don't panic!

The group leader doesn't have to know all the answers. If there are things that you don't know or questions that you can't answer, that's OK! It might be helpful to have a Bible commentary or handbook available so that you can check out any tricky questions. And you can always make a note to ask someone for help and report back to the group.

....do make sure everyone has a chance to contribute.
The leader will need to make sure that quieter people are able to join in the group discussions as well as more noisy ones. The leader will also make sure that it's not always the same people who are asked to share their answers or read out the stories.

....don't dominate!
The group belongs to everyone and everyone should be able to contribute. It's your job to make sure they can. Don't allow the group to be dominated by one person....especially if that person is yourself! If you are an adult leader of a teenage group you will need to be particularly careful to make sure that everyone is allowed to make their own discoveries and move at their own pace.

....do keep things moving.
It's your job to get the group together at the start of the session, and to decide how long to spend on each section. Gently make sure that everyone knows where the session is going. 'I think it's time we moved on now.' 'We'll have two minutes in pairs now, then we'll come together to discuss our answers.' 'Does anyone mind if we skip this next question?'

Notes for each track

Theme
The tracks in this book ask the questions How can I grow in my relationship with God? How can I get to know him better? Introduce this theme to your group before you begin the book.

Here are some notes to help you plan for each group meeting.

Track 1
Why bother with the Bible?
This track looks at the place of the Bible in a Christian's life. If your group are strangers to the Bible take the opportunity to show them one and explain a little about it. The *Play* section gives you an opportunity to explain the difference between the Old and New testaments. You could have several different versions to show, and also a variety of Bible notes and other aids to understanding.

If your group members don't know each other particularly well yet why not play 'Who are you?' from the *Meeting points* section.

Load This section aims to explore what group members feel about the Bible. If the members of your group are very familiar with the Bible already you might want to spend less time on this section and longer on the *Play* section. Perhaps you could just look at the first question and one of the last two questions in this section.

Play If your group is new to Serendipity you will need to explain how the *Play* section works. (See 'How to use this book'.)

Give about ten minutes for people to read through the Bible passages by themselves or in pairs. Encourage them to use a pencil to make whatever jottings they want to. This may mean just a few question marks, or perhaps bits underlined. Then with the whole group together read through the passages, and ask everyone to share the things that they have marked. Talk together about some of the things that arise. Talk about some of the questions we've marked too, but don't feel you have to look at all of them.

Fast forward Use this section to help the group explore ways they might read the Bible. If you are pushed for time, leave out the 'What will you do ?' question.

Be sensitive if you are asking people to share things that they have written in the 'solo' section. Never force people to share what they have written.

Tough talking These questions, like all the others, are optional. Only attempt them if you feel your group would really benefit from a tough discussion.

Pause The reading could be used as a simple act of worship by groups that are not used to praying together. If your group want Bible reading notes but don't know where to start, you could write to Scripture Union (at 130 City Road, London EC1V 2NJ) for information on the notes which they publish.

Track 2
What's the use of praying ?
This track looks at some of the whys and hows of praying. 'Word famine' would be a good *Meeting point* to start this session.

Load The *Load* section is a time for group members to talk about their own experiences and feelings. Many people find prayer difficult to talk about. So make sure that you are positive about everyone's contribution and be careful not to let anyone feel put down.

Track 3
What about other gods ?
There is a baffling number of cults and religions vying for young people's attention. We must take them seriously and not dismiss them lightly. This track aims to help young people to discriminate between the claims of various religious groups.

If you agreed to pray for each other at the end of the last track don't forget to report back.

Track 4
What can I do for God ?
Evangelism is not the only way we can please God. This track looks at some of the many ways we can serve him.

Play It may help to suggest the word 'service' as an alternative for 'fasting' in the first line of the Isaiah passage.

Pause Serving God in practical ways is a kind of worship. Try to choose small situations in which your group could make a real difference. Pray together, and report back to the group next time you meet.

Track 5
Am I ready to pass the message on ?
This track is about passing on the good news about Jesus. Sometimes we call this 'evangelism'.

If you agreed to pray for each other at the end of the last track don't forget to report back !

Load If you think your group could handle it, why not role-play the conversation between Simon and Lenny, using the questions as a starting point. You could even continue the conversation and see what happens next.

Fast forward You will need plenty of time if you are going to write notes to each member of the group, but it can be a very encouraging exercise. Bear in mind that not everyone finds writing easy. You must insist that only encouraging messages are sent. If you feel this exercise wouldn't work for your group, try to find a simpler way for group members to affirm one another.

Track 6
What's my God like ?

This track is designed to help group members explore where they are with God as they finish the book. Try to help people to explore honestly what pictures they have of God, and what feelings they have towards him. To do this you may have to resist the temptation to correct pictures that you think are wrong. See this as a listening session.

Load The question 'What's my God like?' may seem strange. Encourage group members to use plenty of imagination and don't take it *too* seriously !

Play Remember that these questions are for you to choose from. Don't attempt them all.

The passage from Isaiah refers to a vision he had about 750 years before Christ. The Psalm is probably even older.

Fast forward Who usually decides what your group will do next? Try to make sure that the group members themselves have a large say in planning their activities. Then they will be more likely to support them and learn from them.

Keep in touch with Serendipity

Serendipity is more than just a brand name for this book of group meetings. We exist to provide all sorts of help for those who work with young people or adults: Bible study outlines, resource evenings, training for leaders of small groups. If you would like us to keep you posted with news of future books and events, cut out this box and send it to us.

NAME ....

ADDRESS ....

....

....

I am particularly interested in:

youth groups .... {tick as
adult groups .... {appropriate

Send to: Serendipity UK, 48 Peterborough Road, London SW6 3EB